# THE TEMPTATIONS OF JESUS

## Six Dramas For Lent

### BY CURT M. JOSEPH

C.S.S. Publishing Co., Inc.
Lima, Ohio

THE TEMPTATIONS OF JESUS

Copyright © 1993 by
The C.S.S. Publishing Company, Inc.
Lima, Ohio

All rights reserved. No part of this publication may be reproduced, stored in a retrieval system, or transmitted in any form or by any means, electronic, mechanical, photocopying, recording, or otherwise, without the prior permission of the publisher. Inquiries should be addressed to: The C.S.S. Publishing Company, Inc., 628 South Main Street, Lima, Ohio 45804.

---

**Library of Congress Cataloging-in-Publication Data**

Joseph, Curt M., 1949-
    The temptations of Jesus : six dramas for Lent / by Curt M. Joseph.
    67 p.    14 by 21.5 cm.
    ISBN 1-55673-562-6
    1. Jesus Christ—Drama. 2. Christian drama, American. 3. Lent. I. Title
PS3560.07725T46    1993
812'.54—dc20                                                     92-32271
                                                                                                              CIP

---

9309 / ISBN 1-55673-562-6                                       PRINTED IN U.S.A.

This is dedicated to my parents, Bill and Lorraine. From my dad I learned the importance of responsibility and being a "stand up guy," a good explanation of the "infield fly rule," and the concept of grace as a free unearned gift. I learned that when he bought me a pair of baseball spikes that I did not deserve.

From my mom I learned compassion, understanding, tolerance and to respect every human being no matter who they were. And if that weren't enough she made the best chocolate milkshake in the world.

Thanks for being my parents and I only hope that I have been worthy of all the time and effort you put into raising me.

Curt

# **Table Of Contents**

Introduction                          7

Drama One                         11

Drama Two                         21

Drama Three                      31

Drama Four                        41

Drama Five                         51

Drama Six                           61

# Introduction

Webster defines the word "temptation" in this way: "The act of tempting or state of being tempted; an enticement to evil; that which is presented as an inducement, enticement or allurement."

As we enter the season of Lent our minds are filled with many different thoughts and images. One of the thoughts that stands out for me is the humanity of Jesus. Jesus was indeed God, but he was also very human, and if the God/Jesus were to ever understand the human condition he had to endure all that you and I have to endure. The joys, the pain, the struggles and the temptations of life.

These six dramas try to capture the difficulty that Jesus endured. Matthew and Luke record in detail the first temptations of Jesus when he encounters Satan in the wilderness area beyond the Jordan. But were these the only times that Jesus was tempted? After all Luke wrote, "After Satan had tempted Jesus in every way, he left him for a little while." All of us can overcome temptations from time to time. That is part of being human. So, Satan felt that he would be able to tempt Jesus at another time and in another place.

The first three dramas are all based on the Temptation of Jesus as written in Matthew 4:1-11.

The fourth drama is based on John 6:1-15. Here John recounts how Jesus fed the 5,000 and in response the people wanted to make him an earthly king. John says Jesus withdrew into the hills to pray. Certainly Jesus was tempted to take the easy way. The way of earthly power and glory. How tempted Jesus must have been to give in when thousands wanted to make him their king.

The fifth drama is based on the story of Jesus in the Garden of Gethsemane in Luke 22:39-46. No one wants to die, not even Jesus. All humans prize and cherish life and Jesus was no different. The temptation that he had to face was that of personal safety or giving himself up for the sake of humanity.

The sixth drama takes place at the foot of the cross. If you remember the temptation stories in Matthew 4 and Luke 4 you will remember that Satan tempted Jesus by saying, "If you are the Son of God . . ." As you recall the crucifixion stories in the gospels you will remember the crowds taunting Jesus with the words, "If you are God's son, come down from there." Satan did indeed return at a more opportune time.

What I find so intriguing about all of these stories is that the human Jesus does not call on his divine powers to overcome these temptations. To defeat temptation he uses his faith in God, the scriptures and prayer. We too can defeat temptation if we have faith in God alone, rely on the word of God and come to God in prayer.

Insofar as staging I have written these dramas with a minimum of staging and stage directions. These plays then are workable in large congregations or very small congregations.

I have always felt that in the biblical dramas that I have written, the dress and language of the actors should be contemporary. I feel that way because it stresses the timelessness of the biblical story. These stories are as relevant today as they were 2,000 years ago.

When we performed these dramas at Highland Park Lutheran Church in Des Moines, Iowa, the fellow who played the part of Jesus was a carpenter. He wore his overalls, work boots and flannel shirts.

Satan on the other hand was always neatly dressed sometimes in a three-piece suit with derby hat and walking stick and at other times in a flashy sports coat, bow tie and straw hat.

Some pastors and lay people are not to be excited by liturgical drama, but if one looks at the Bible, one sees that there is high drama from Genesis through Revelation.

Drama is also good in that it includes more people than just the pastor in the worship service. And anytime we can include more people in worship I think we have done something worthwhile.

I have enjoyed writing, acting and directing these dramas and I hope that you will get as much out of them as I have.

> Curt M. Joseph, pastor
> Highland Park Lutheran Church
> Des Moines, Iowa

# Drama One

No staging is needed. The drama takes place in the wilderness area outside of Jerusalem. It is based on Matthew 4:1-4.

**Characters:**

**Jesus of Nazareth:** early 30s. He is dressed very casually. He could be wearing blue jeans and similar casual clothes.

**Satan:** He is neatly dressed, wearing a flashy three-piece suit. He could have a walking stick and derby or straw hat.

The drama opens with Jesus off to the side of the stage, almost out of sight. He sits there in prayer or in meditation. After a few moments he is joined on stage by Satan. He enters the stage a little tired and looking around as though he is looking for something or someone.

**Satan:** What a horrible place. God-forsaken territory. I don't know how anything could survive out here. I don't know why this little encounter had to take place out here. Next time I am going to choose the location. I can certainly find something better than this.

**Jesus:** *(He looks up.)* Good afternoon. It is afternoon, isn't it?

**Satan:** *(He looks at his watch.)* Yes, about 12:30 actually.

**Jesus:** It's kind of nice to see another person. I've been out here so long, I've kind of forgotten what people look like. May I help you?

**Satan:** Don't suppose so.

**Jesus:** You seem to be looking for something or someone.

**Satan:** If you must know, I'm looking for someone. Young chap. Late 20s, early 30s. *(Jesus gets up and walks toward Satan. As he does, Satan looks Jesus over very carefully.)* Rugged fellow, carpenter by trade. Comes from up north, near Nazareth I believe. In fact you could be the one.

**Jesus:** I could be. Depends.

**Satan:** What are you out here for? Such a horrible place. I'm from out of town. Does this place have a name?

**Jesus:** Yes, people from around here call it the "Devil's Playground," or the "Devil's Anvil." Sometimes it gets so hot on this flat rocky stretch that people think it's kind of like standing on an anvil. I don't suppose you'd know anything about the devil.

**Satan:** Well, I know that none of his playgrounds look like this. They are a lot more attractive than this. I don't believe I caught your name. *(He extends his hand.)*

**Jesus:** *(They shake.)* Jesus. Jesus of Nazareth.

**Satan:** Well, I'll be da. . . *(He looks him over very carefully.)*

**Jesus:** I didn't catch your name.

**Satan:** Oh, I go by many different names. Let's see, "Ol' Scratch," "The Prince of Darkness," "Lucifer," "Beelzebub." I hate that one. It makes me sounds like some kind of insect. I guess most people know me as Satan, the accuser.

**Jesus:** I guess I've been expecting you.

**Satan:** So you are the one I'm suppose to meet. I kind of wondered if you weren't.

**Jesus:** You're not at all like I expected.

**Satan:** And just what did you expect?

**Jesus:** Someone who looked a bit more evil, sinister; with a black cape and all.

**Satan:** *(He laughs.)* I just love it. When people talk about me like that, when they imagine that's what I look like, I just love it. They think I'm going to look like some villain out of an old-time movie.

**Jesus:** What?

**Satan:** Forget it dear boy. They like to dress me up in a red union suit, put horns on my head and give me a pitchfork. I love it. Who could take anyone dressed like that seriously? And that's what I want. I don't want anyone to take me seriously. That's when I work the best.

**Jesus:** Well, I just thought you would be different.

**Satan:** You have a great deal to learn. I look different to everyone. To the man over there, I can be the most beautiful woman in the world. To the woman over there I can be a bottle of liquor. To the man over there I can be a sack full of money. To the lady over there I can be hedonistic pleasure. I can look different to different people. I can look like whatever it is they desire most. That's part of my charm. And the beautiful part is that up to this moment I have always looked too good to pass up.

**Jesus:** What do you mean this moment?

**Satan:** Don't tell me the Father has been keeping you in the dark?

**Jesus:** I don't know what you mean.

**Satan:** Yes, that's part of God's charm. He likes to keep a few little secrets to himself. That's what started it all, you know.

**Jesus:** Started what?

**Satan:** For some reason the Father always enjoyed keeping his loyal angels in the dark. I believed that if he wanted true loyalty from us, he should have shared all his knowledge. When he wouldn't do that, well, I thought it was time we went our separate ways.

**Jesus:** I see.

**Satan:** Anyway, up until now, I have always had my way with people. Adam and Eve, David and Bathsheba, and the list could go on and on. Anyway, my good fellow, this whole confrontation was set up by the Father.

**Jesus:** God set this up?

**Satan:** You are either a very good little actor, or you really are in the dark. Makes no mind. You will give in before it's all over. The Holy Spirit led you out here.

**Jesus:** Why?

**Satan:** Because God had to see what you're made of.

**Jesus:** So, God wanted to see what I'm made of?

**Satan:** Irritating, isn't he? Kind of makes you angry doesn't it?

**Jesus:** No, I just don't understand.

**Satan:** *(He laughs.)* I know this is a set up. You're not even human are you? *(He reaches out and pinches Jesus.)*

**Jesus:** Ouch!

**Satan:** I guess you are human.

**Jesus:** Of course I'm human. Why wouldn't I be human?

**Satan:** Look at it this way. Pretend two men are wagering on the outcome of a contest. The bet is pretty heavy. In fact, the ruination of one of the two hangs in the balance. In order to get a little advantage, to get a little better odds, one of the two throws in a ringer.

**Jesus:** Yes, I see.

**Satan:** I just thought maybe the old boy had thrown in a ringer. But you are human.

**Jesus:** Yes, I'm very human and very hungry.

**Satan:** Hungry? Why?

**Jesus:** If you had been out here for 40 days without a thing to eat, you'd be hungry, too.

**Satan:** You haven't had a thing to eat in 40 days?

**Jesus:** Nothing.

**Satan:** This is going to be easier than I thought.

**Jesus:** What do you mean?

**Satan:** Don't get so excited. This is going to be like falling off a log. *(He picks up a stone.)* Here, take a bite.

**Jesus:** *(He takes the stone out of Satan's hand.)* This is a rock. If I bite into this, I'll break one of my teeth.

**Satan:** No you won't. All you have to do is say the right words and it will turn into a nice piece of fresh baked bread. Go ahead, it's easier than you think.

**Jesus:** I can't.

**Satan:** Don't be ridiculous. Go ahead.

**Jesus:** I told you I can't.

**Satan:** *(Angry.)* What do you mean, you can't?

**Jesus:** I mean I can't.

**Satan:** Look, are you trying to tell me that the Son of God, the one through whom the world was created, can't change this rock into a piece of bread?

**Jesus:** No, I can't. Believe me, I wish I could. But I can't.

**Satan:** Of course you can. In a few days you are going to turn water into wine, calm storms, heal the sick, feed 5,000 and raise people from the dead. So don't tell me that you can't do this.

**Jesus:** I can, but I can't.

**Satan:** Why not? If you can do all that other stuff, then it would seem to me you could use your divine powers to change this little rock into a moldy old piece of bread.

**Jesus:** If you are asking, "Do I have the power to change this rock into a piece of bread," the answer is "Yes." If you are asking, "Will I use my power to change this into bread," the answer is "No."

**Satan:** Why not?

**Jesus:** Before I came down here the Father and I had a long talk. He said that if I consented to his plan, I had to deal with life like any other human. That I could not use my divine powers. And I agreed. I decided that I would be obedient to the Father's Word, no matter what.

**Satan:** No matter what?

**Jesus:** Yes, food is not the only thing that gives life. A person must have God's Word. A person can sit down to a banquet, but if he does not know God's Word he will come away hungry, no matter how much he has eaten. People don't live by bread alone, but they live by God's Word.

**Satan:** Wait a minute. If you agreed not to use your divine powers, how are you going to turn water into wine, heal the sick and raise people from the dead?

**Jesus:** I guess I left out one small detail.

**Satan:** Just one small detail, huh?

**Jesus:** Yes, the Father and I agreed that I could not use my divine powers for my own needs. But I could use them whenever I wanted to, for the needs of others. Feeding people, healing them, raising people from the dead, that all falls under the category of helping others, and it's okay. No harm, no sin.

**Satan:** Go ahead, no one will see you.

**Jesus:** It's really not important who sees me or not. What's important is that I know I will have broken the Father's Word.

**Satan:** To thine own self be true, huh?

**Jesus:** I guess. Besides there's another reason I can't turn this into bread.

**Satan:** What's that?

**Jesus:** There are thousands of people dying of starvation in this world. In fact, before this day is over, 10,000 will die of starvation. It is important that I know what those people are going through. It is important that I feel their pain, that I know their fear. Not one of them can say the words and turn stones into bread. And the only way God's plan of salvation will work is if we both know what people are going through.

**Satan:** Is that your final word?

**Jesus:** No, that's God's final word.

**Satan:** Okay kid, not bad. But we have a long way to go.

**Jesus:** What do you mean?

**Satan:** I mean this was just the first round. We were just kind of feeling each other out. From here on in we get serious.

**Jesus:** Serious?

**Satan:** Yes, there's too much at stake.

**Jesus:** Yes, you're right. The whole world is at stake.

**Satan:** That's right, kid. We're just beginning. Follow me. The second round is about to begin.

# Drama Two

No special effects are needed. The drama can be done in the middle of the chancel. The drama takes place on the roof of the temple.

**Characters:**

**Jesus:** early 30s, casually dressed, could be wearing blue jeans and work clothes.

**Satan:** neatly dressed. He wears a three-piece suit. He may wear a derby or straw hat and he could carry a walking stick.

This drama begins with Satan leading Jesus on stage.

**Satan:** Well, here we are. What do you think? Beautiful view, don't you agree?

**Jesus:** Yes, magnificent.

**Satan:** Of course, anything would be better than being out in the middle of the wilderness.

**Jesus:** That's for sure.

**Satan:** The world sure looks different from the top of the temple.

**Jesus:** Just how high up are we?

**Satan:** Do heights bother you?

**Jesus:** Not at all. I was just wondering how far up we are. I would guess we are about 500, maybe 550, feet in the air.

**Satan:** Not a bad guess. Actually, we are just a couple of feet over 600 feet in the air.

**Jesus:** 600 feet in the air, huh?

**Satan:** Are you sure heights don't bother you?

**Jesus:** No, no, not at all. I was just taken in by how different things look from up here. Just a different vantage point. The people look smaller. It's almost like looking down at some ants scurrying here and there.

**Satan:** Yes, and where are they rushing to? To their own graves, that's where. They're not enjoying life. They're not really living, they're just existing.

**Jesus:** Why do you say that?

**Satan:** None of them really understands what life is all about.

**Jesus:** And you do?

**Satan:** Of course I do. I invented life.

**Jesus:** That's strange. I thought the Father was the one who brought life into the world.

**Satan:** No, he brought existence into the world. I taught people how to live, how to enjoy life. Living for the moment, grabbing for the brass ring whenever it passes by. That's what life is all about.

**Jesus:** That's a pretty pessimistic view of life isn't it?

**Satan:** Not really. If anything, I'd say it's realistic.

**Jesus:** Don't be ridiculous.

**Satan:** No really. Think about it. You are brought into this world and from there it's just a matter of being in the right place and the right time. And then one day it all ends. They cart you off to the cemetery, throw some dirt on you, lay a few pieces of sod over you, and that's it. So, you might as well get all you can in this life.

**Jesus:** But what about life after here?

**Satan:** You mean heaven and hell and all that?

**Jesus:** Exactly.

**Satan:** Well, as far as I'm concerned, that kind of talk is bad for business. Ignorance is bliss. What they don't know, won't hurt them.

**Jesus:** In other words, don't tell them the truth.

**Satan:** Do you really think they want to know the truth? By and large, people are only concerned about what happens here. They don't even think about the next life.

**Jesus:** But they should. We're talking about two different kinds of life after it's all over here.

**Satan:** Sure, sure. What you have to offer is eternity floating on some cloud. What I have to offer is the lake of fire and all that good old brimstone.

**Jesus:** That's ridiculous. That's not what eternity is all about.

**Satan:** You're right, but you see my objective is to get people not to think about it. Now this lake of fire business is unbelievable. It sounds like some made up fairy tale. And no one believes in fairy tales. I lull people into a false sense of security. I'm happy when people talk about fire and brimstone, because if people knew what hell was really like, well, you'd have to put an additional wing on heaven to make room for all the extra folks. As long as I can make a joke out of it all, then I win.

**Jesus:** Tell me, what is hell really like?

**Satan:** You can't imagine. Words can't really describe it. You think this is a dog eat dog world, you ought to see hell.

**Jesus:** I think I'll pass,

**Satan:** Just give me time. Anyway, imagine that you've gone to some kind of gathering. A party let's say. And you arrive, and everything looks great. But then suddenly you realize that no one is talking to anyone else. That no one really cares about anyone else. That no one wants to have anything to do with you. No one wants to get to know you. No one wants to try and understand you. That's what hell is like. And believe me, that's worse, far worse, than all the fire and brimstone put together.

**Jesus:** And heaven, the kingdom is just the opposite.

**Satan:** That's right, but the question is which place is going to fill up first. You know, the two of us are really nothing more than public relations men for the places we represent. You're trying to recruit people and so am I. The problem for you is that I am doing a much better job at it than you are.

**Jesus:** You are?

**Satan:** Are you kidding? I've got them waiting in line. If you'd like I could give you a few pointers.

**Jesus:** You're going to give me pointers?

**Satan:** Sure. Actually, I've done some marketing research. People want to be associated with winners. They want to be successes. They want it all in life. Happiness, pleasure, ease, comfort, security. That's what you have to appeal to. Give people what they want or at least promise them what they want and they will follow you anywhere.

**Jesus:** All right, if you were the Messiah, what would do?

**Satan:** You know, if the Father had given me that job years ago, I never would have left him. But there is no sense in crying over spilled milk. I would work to influence and impress people.

**Jesus:** What do you mean?

**Satan:** First I would dress for success. Clothes do make the man. Then I would do some great things. A few corporate takeovers. Let them know you are a high roller. Make people want to follow you. I have seen your game plan and frankly I am a little disappointed. I mean this serving, suffering and dying business went out with the prophetic movement about 400 years ago. The world has changed, my friend. That's the problem with God, he hasn't changed. He was, he is and he always will be the same. Give it up, it's a bad plan.

**Jesus:** But it's God's plan.

**Satan:** And I'm telling you, that it's got some serious flaws. I mean really, you start telling people if they're going to follow you they have to be willing to serve, suffer and die. That's not the best way to win friends and influence people. Go with the dramatic, the spectacular. It is so much easier than what God has planned for you.

**Jesus:** But I have always trusted the Father.

**Satan:** Trust me, the Father dealt you a lousy hand. Look, do you know that if you follow God's way, at the end you are not only going to die, but you are going to die alone. Abandoned, forgotten by everyone. They are going to crucify you on the town garbage dump. They're going to toss you out like so much garbage. And those who trusted you the most, your best friends, are going to run out on you. Do you want to die alone?

**Jesus:** Of course not.

**Satan:** Do you know what it is like to die on a cross? It is horrible. It is a slow and agonizing way to go. The pain will drive you insane. You hang there until you either die of suffocation or cardiac arrest. I've seen people take up to three and four days dying on the cross. Believe me, that's not the way to go.

**Jesus:** Then what should I do?

**Satan:** Look, it's 2:55. People are starting to flock to the temple for afternoon prayers. There will be a good crowd down there. Two, three thousand people. Now here's my plan. At 2:59 all you have to do is jump off of here. It says in the Psalms that God will protect you from even stubbing your toe. So, jump and you will float down like a feather. The folks will eat it up. They'll know for sure that you are the Son of God. No big deal for a man like you.

**Jesus:** Jump?

**Satan:** Sure, jump. Unless you are afraid that God will let you down. Or maybe you're not sure if you are God's son. How terrible to jump, not knowing for sure if you're God's son or not. How terrible to go through life not knowing if you are God's son. Pretty rough way to live. Take the easy way kid. You can do it. Have faith.

**Jesus:** Have faith, huh?

**Satan:** Sure, sure, have faith. Why, if you have the faith of a mustard seed, you can jump down from here without getting hurt. Go ahead. Put the old man's money where his mouth is. God has been making all these wonderful promises, make him come through on just one. I'll tell you what. If you jump, if you land safely, I'll even start believing again. Come on, that's a pretty good deal.

**Jesus:** You know, you have just about convinced me. And that business with quoting scripture, that was a nice touch. But the Word of God says not to put God to the test.

**Satan:** That's because if God were put to the test he'd fail and let everyone down.

**Jesus:** There's nothing you won't stop at. You are out to destroy the whole world.

**Satan:** Look, if you follow God's plan completely, then I'm lost. And if I'm going down, I'm going to take as many with me as I can.

**Jesus:** Why?

**Satan:** Because I know how that will hurt the Father. I know that even the loss of one of his creation hurts him deeply. So, if I can take millions, even billions of people with me, it will break his heart. It's called evening the score.

**Jesus:** That's right, that will break the Father's heart. Because God loves each and every person he has ever created, including you. And that is why God sent me. To show the world that serving, suffering and dying are the best of all possible ways to live.

**Satan:** You're really tough.

**Jesus:** Not me. The Word. God's Word is tough. That is where I find my strength. That is where I find my courage. That is where I find the faith to go on. I find all that I need in the Word. The Word keeps me in balance. It gives me direction. It gives me a reason to live. You see, without the Word I am just another lost person looking for a way out. But with the Word, I know the way. The problem is that too many of God's people don't know his Word. And in not knowing his Word, they have lost everything, including their lives.

**Satan:** Not bad. You're giving me a run for my money. But that's the way I like it. The harder the task the more I enjoy it when I win in the end.

**Jesus:** Well, you haven't done too well so far.

**Satan:** It's still in the early innings. I'm only down by two and more importantly than that, look at my record. I've never lost. Follow me, I think we can clear this up shortly. *(They walk off together.)*

# Drama Three

**Characters:**

**Jesus:** Casually dressed, can be in work clothes.

**Satan:** Neatly dressed, three-piece suit or blazer, hat and walking stick.

This drama opens with both men walking out on the stage. As they walk to center stage, both of them are looking around as tourists, seeing some magnificent scenery for the first time. Jesus is the more impressed of the two. When they get to center stage, Jesus continues to look around until Satan speaks.

**Satan:** Magnificent, don't you agree?

**Jesus:** I have never seen anything that rivals this. It's breathtaking.

**Satan:** Yes, there were a few things that the old boy did right. He sure knew what he was doing when he created the world. Unfortunately he didn't know how to relate to angels or people too well. But that's all over and done with.

**Jesus:** From up here it's like I can see forever.

**Satan:** You can, my dear boy. Drink it all in. Don't be shy, revel in the beauty of it all.

**Jesus:** I just can't get over it.

**Satan:** Impressive, huh?

**Jesus:** *(Jesus looks off to the east.)* Impressive isn't the word for it. What direction am I facing?

**Satan:** East, my dear boy.

**Jesus:** What am I looking at?

**Satan:** Well, let's see, that's Saudi Arabia, Iraq, Iran, India, Russia, China, Korea and Japan.

**Jesus:** Those are rather strange names. I've never heard of them before.

**Satan:** Some of them are not even nations yet. But one day they will make up the middle and far east. The area is rich with oil, rubber, and other resources. Nations will go to war just for the right to trade with those countries. The person in charge of all of that will be quite a respected person.

**Jesus:** *(Jesus turns to the north.)* Let's see if that's east, then this must be north.

**Satan:** Correct. Now that's Turkey, Greece, Eastern Europe. Wonderful part of the world.

**Jesus:** Looks beautiful.

**Satan:** So beautiful that rulers will sell out their own family members, will assassinate rival kings and queens and go to war to possess that land.

**Jesus:** *(Jesus turns to the west.)* And what is that to the west?

**Satan:** Europe. Rome, Berlin, Paris, the British Isles and beyond that, the United States. Lands rich with human and natural resources. The person who controls all of that, literally controls the destiny of the world.

**Jesus:** I see. *(He turns to the south.)* Now let's see what is that to the south.

**Satan:** Africa. Diamonds, oil and all the slave labor imaginable. *(Jesus slowly turns around and looks at it all again.)* You really like it, I can tell.

**Jesus:** What's not to like?

**Satan:** It can be all yours, just say the word.

**Jesus:** *(He laughs.)* What do you mean, "all mine?"

**Satan:** Exactly what I said, "all yours." It is within my power to give all of this to you.

**Jesus:** What do you mean? All this belongs to God.

**Satan:** Not exactly. When the Father and I went our separate ways he remained in heaven and I took out a sublease on hell and the world. Long term, ironclad lease. It's mine. I can do with it as I wish. It's kind of like my toy. Some kids get toy soldiers to play with, I get real soldiers to play with. It's fun. You can't imagine.

**Jesus:** I suppose I can.

**Satan:** No, not really. Why I can promise a little piece of land to a person and there isn't one thing he won't do to obtain or keep that piece of land.

**Jesus:** What do you mean? Give me an example.

**Satan:** You've heard of Herod?

**Jesus:** Antipas?

**Satan:** No, his father, Herod the Great.

**Jesus:** Yes.

**Satan:** Well, Herod the Great was the King of Judea and the surrounding areas. Actually he was only king because Rome let him be king. Anyway, he was so afraid that he would lose that little chunk of land, that he murdered his own mother and two of his sons. He was afraid they were going to try and take the throne from him. Not only that, but if it hadn't been for my old friend, Gabriel, Herod would have gotten you too. He was so afraid of losing his kingdom that when he heard the Messiah had been born in Bethlehem, he had all the male children under two years old murdered. You got away because Gabriel told your father to take you to Egypt. That's just one example. I could give you more.

**Jesus:** It is a sad world when men will sacrifice anything for a few square miles of land. That's what I came to change.

**Satan:** And I am here to tell you, you are wasting your time. The world and the people in it will never change.

**Jesus:** I am here to show them that there is another way.

**Satan:** Wake up, young man. There is only one way. The way of power, force and violence. MY WAY!

**Jesus:** There is another way.

**Satan:** No, there isn't. When I took out the sub-lease on this place, I made it mine. I make the rules. Everyone answers to me. Everyone does it my way or they don't play the game.

**Jesus:** And just how do you play the game?

**Satan:** It's easier than you think. Anyway, back to the original point. This can all be yours, just say the word.

**Jesus:** And what is the word?

**Satan:** All you have to do is worship me.

**Jesus:** Worship you, huh?

**Satan:** See, I told you it was no big deal. You don't even have to get down on your knees. Just a slight bowing of the head. That's all, nothing to it.

**Jesus:** Just bow down to you, that's all, huh?

**Satan:** That's all. Very simple. You will be the most powerful, most exalted person in the world. It'll be yours forever.

**Jesus:** What do you mean forever?

**Satan:** I mean, until my lease expires.

**Jesus:** Why are you offering this to me?

**Satan:** Because I like you. You're a nice kid. This could be the start of a great friendship.

**Jesus:** I think I'll pass.

**Satan:** Don't be ridiculous. This is an offer no one can refuse.

**Jesus:** I can.

**Satan:** Why?

**Jesus:** Because I don't need what you have.

**Satan:** Listen, a lot of people have felt that way, will feel that way, but in the end I always win out.

**Jesus:** Not this time.

**Satan:** Just who do you think you are? Pharaohs, kings, emperors, have all sold out for what I have to offer. Alexander the Great, Genghis Kahn, the Caesars, to name just a few. And there will be many more. People like Napoleon, Peter the Great, Mussolini, Stalin, Hitler. All of them will reach out and grab for the greatness. Why are you any different than they are?

**Jesus:** Because one day it will all be mine anyway. It's just a matter of time.

**Satan:** Time, time. Why do you have to wait? Why should anyone have to wait for power, riches, fame and fortune? You can have it all now. Just reach out and take it. Don't be a fool. Take it now.

**Jesus:** One day it will be mine, and it will be mine forever, not just until the lease runs out.

**Satan:** But at what price?

**Jesus:** What price?

**Satan:** If you want it now, all you have to do is bow your head. If you do it God's way, you are talking about suffering and death. Is that the price you want to pay?

**Jesus:** No one WANTS to pay that price, but I will because that is what the Father wants.

**Satan:** And what do you want?

**Jesus:** I want the will of the Father to be done in the world.

**Satan:** You are disgusting. You're a fool. Just bow down, that's all.

**Jesus:** The Word of God says . . .

**Satan:** FORGET THE WORD OF GOD!

**Jesus:** says to worship God and God alone.

**Satan:** You are crazy. You are certifiable, you know that.

**Jesus:** I am obedient to the Will of God.

**Satan:** I have offered far less to others and they have taken my offer with no questions asked. Why not you?

**Jesus:** Because there are really more important things in the world than power, fame and glory.

**Satan:** What is more important than that?

**Jesus:** Human beings. I have not come to destroy human beings, I have come to love them, to serve them and to die for them. And that is more important than anything in the world.

**Satan:** You are a fool.

**Jesus:** And you are afraid.

**Satan:** Afraid of what?

**Jesus:** Afraid that if I carry through with the Father's plan, your lease will run out a lot sooner than you thought. You're scared because you know that if I go to the cross, if I follow the Father's will, God will be victorious and you will be defeated.

**Satan:** This is crazy. You're crazy if you think by dying you will beat me.

**Jesus:** If that is not the case, then why are you so afraid of me? Why are you trying so hard to keep me from following God's plan?

**Satan:** I told you I like you, that's all.

**Jesus:** You are a liar, you are the father of lies. You must keep me from the cross, or you are finished.

**Satan:** Just forget it then. *(He starts to leave.)* I'll offer it to someone who is smarter than you.

**Jesus:** You mean it's over.

**Satan:** What's over?

**Jesus:** This testing business.

**Satan:** *(He laughs.)* Not by a long shot. I'll be back at a more opportune time. I'll be back when your defenses are down, when you are not feeling holier than thou. *(He walks off.)* I'll get you, if it's the last thing I ever do. *(Jesus walks off in the opposite direction.)*

# Drama Four

**Characters:**

**Jesus:** Early 30s, dressed casually in blue jeans, although he is neat and clean.

**Satan:** Neatly dressed. He can wear a three-piece suit and bowler hat, or sports jacket and straw hat. He carries a walking stick.

The drama opens with Satan sitting on stage. After a few moments Jesus comes on stage. He looks tired, he sits and sighs, and does not know Satan is present until Satan speaks.

**Satan:** Well, I've been expecting you. Looks like you've put in a long day.

**Jesus:** *(He laughs.)* You again. As I was coming out here, I had this feeling that I wasn't alone. I should have known you'd be here.

**Satan:** You look exhausted. You look hungry too. *(He takes an apple out of his pocket and takes a bite.)* I can see why they call these delicious. Would you like a bite?

**Jesus:** *(He thinks for a moment.)* No thanks, I'll pass. Although it does look good.

**Satan:** Are you sure? *(He offers the apple.)*

**Jesus:** Yes, I'm sure.

**Satan:** Well, it's worked before. Can't blame a guy for trying. It's been a long time since we've seen each other. How are things going?

**Jesus:** I'm not sure. There are those who will follow me anywhere and there are others, who, uh, won't even give me a chance. Sometimes I wonder if I am saying, if I'm doing the right things.

**Satan:** I know just what you mean. Convincing people to follow me is tough work too, you know. Sometimes they're beating down the doors, and the next day, not a soul in sight. It's either feast or famine.

**Jesus:** I'm just not sure.

**Satan:** Security, happiness and comfort, that's what people want. Offer them that and they will follow you anywhere.

**Jesus:** Yes, I know what you mean. Today was a perfect example of that.

**Satan:** Oh? What happened?

**Jesus:** Well, I had just finished healing a great many people. All manner of sickness, disease, paralysis, possession.

**Satan:** Yes, I've heard. My people tell me that you can be pretty rough on them during an exorcism.

**Jesus:** I'm sorry.

**Satan:** Hey, ask no quarter, give no quarter. Anyway, continue.

**Jesus:** Anyway, I had healed a great many people. My disciples and I went across the lake to get away from the crowds. We were all exhausted. But they followed us. They kept pressing in on us, demanding more and more.

**Satan:** Pushy lot.

**Jesus:** No, not really. Just plain folks who for the first time in their lives, saw some hope. Anyway, they followed me up a hill. They had been following me all day and the hour was late. The people were starved and it was too late to go and buy food at the town market.

**Satan:** I'm getting the picture.

**Jesus:** Their need for food was overwhelming.

**Satan:** And what did you do about it?

**Jesus:** I met their need. There was a young boy, about nine, 10, maybe 11. Anyway, he had a small sack. And in the sack were five small loaves and two dried fish.

**Satan:** Then what?

**Jesus:** Well, first I asked the apostles for help, but they couldn't.

**Satan:** Dull lot that you picked. So plain, so, so ordinary.

**Jesus:** Then I asked the boy for his food and he gladly gave it to me. I thanked God for it and asked him to fulfill the needs of the people. And he did.

**Satan:** AMAZING!

**Jesus:** Just like when God fed his people in the wilderness during the time of Moses and the Exodus.

**Satan:** How did you do it?

**Jesus:** I'm not sure. Actually, I didn't do it. God did it. I just asked for his help. That's how it always works.

**Satan:** TRULY AMAZING! Now, how did you really do it?

**Jesus:** I told you, I didn't do it. God did it.

**Satan:** Come on dear boy, enough of this false humility. Fess up, how did you do it?

**Jesus:** You don't understand. It's just what happens when someone turns his life over to God. Fantastic, wonderful things happen.

**Satan:** That's easy for you to say, you're divine.

**Jesus:** But I am a human being. I just turn everything over to God. I trust God completely. I have all the confidence, all the trust, all the faith in the world in God. And when anyone has that kind of faith in God, well, wonderful, miraculous things can and do happen.

**Satan:** You mean to tell me that you never rely on yourself?

**Jesus:** Never. I always go to God.

**Satan:** Kind of use him as a crutch, huh? Why don't you stand up and be a man? Take charge of your own life.

**Jesus:** And you know what happens when people try and take charge of their own lives?

**Satan:** What?

**Jesus:** They wind up following you. You see, no human being is strong enough to stand on his own. Every human being needs someone to rely on. And if a person doesn't rely on God, he will wind up relying on you.

**Satan:** Exactly.

**Jesus:** You knew all along, didn't you?

**Satan:** Of course.

**Jesus:** Then why did you ask me?

**Satan:** To plant the seeds of doubt, my dear boy. If I can make you doubt God and trust in yourself, then I win. It's that simple. That's one of the ways I work the best. I plant the seeds of doubt. When someone tells a lie, for example, I am right there to whisper in their ear, "Are you sure God can forgive you?" If someone steals something, I am quick to say, "You know God will never forgive you for that." Doubt, my dear boy, doubt.

**Jesus:** So that is your plan.

**Satan:** And I must say it was working quite well, until you came along. But there is always a fly in the ointment. That is the true measure of greatness. When one faces obstacles, the great ones can overcome them. And I will overcome you as well.

**Jesus:** You think so, huh?

**Satan:** I know so. Anyway, back to the original question. You were wondering how to gain more followers.

**Jesus:** Yes, that was it.

**Satan:** All right, let's debrief what happened today. You healed them, cast out some demons and fed them, correct?

**Jesus:** Correct.

**Satan:** And they were following you everywhere, correct?

**Jesus:** Correct.

**Satan:** In fact, they were ready to do more than follow you, they were ready to make you king. Think of it, "JESUS OF NAZARETH, THE BREAD KING." Catchy title.

**Jesus:** Bread king. Right.

**Satan:** No, seriously. They want a leader who will give them everything they want. Food, comfort, security, happiness. Well, give them what they want. They want a leader of power and strength. They want a leader who will climb upon his valiant white charger and drive the Romans out of town. That's what they want. So give them what they want.

**Jesus:** Give them what they want, huh?

**Satan:** Yes, give them what whey want. Appeal to their most basic instincts. The instinct to survive. The desire to do things the easy way. Appeal to those things. They want a strong powerful king, GIVE THEM A STRONG POWERFUL KING. They deserve it and you owe it to them.

**Jesus:** I don't think so.

**Satan:** Look, you told me that you want to help people, right?

**Jesus:** Right.

**Satan:** What better way to help people than to throw the Romans out by force and to give people the things they want. Seize the moment. Don't blow it. Give them what they want and they will serve you forever.

**Jesus:** But I came not to be served, but to serve. I came to give my life as a ransom for all people.

**Satan:** Look, it will be much simpler and easier if you just throw the Romans out. That's what they want.

**Jesus:** Yes, that's what they want. But what they need is a savior. One who will save them not from Rome, but from their real enemy.

**Satan:** And who is that?

**Satan:** YOU! You are the real enemy of all people. You who would tear down instead of build up. You who would bring death rather than life. You who would enslave rather than set free. You are the enemy of all people. You are what all people need to be saved and set free from. And that is why I came. To teach them the truth. And once they know the truth, the TRUTH WILL SET THEM FREE.

**Satan:** And what is TRUTH?

**Jesus:** The Word of God and nothing else. Everything else is just an illusion. Nothing but God's word is reality. And I am here to tell people just what you are.

**Satan:** And what am I?

**Jesus:** The FATHER OF LIES. You are completely corrupt and twisted. I will defeat you, not with sword, not with earthly power, but with the power of love. A love that will lead me to make the final sacrifice for all people.

**Satan:** Don't bet on it FRIEND. I have broken better men than you. Once you begin to experience the persecution, once you feel the lash on your back, once you feel the spikes tear into your hands and feet, once you stare death in the eye, you will come crawling to me. You'll beg me to spare you.

**Jesus:** I would die before I would crawl to you.

**Satan:** Well, my friend, by the time I'm done with you, you'll wish you were dead, but in the end you'll come around to my way of thinking.

**Jesus:** No I won't.

**Satan:** Would you like to make a little wager?

**Jesus:** A wager?

**Satan:** Yes, I'll bet the eternal spirits of every living human being that in the end you will cave in.

**Jesus:** On my own I cannot beat you. So, in the name of God, the one who freed Israel, who parted the Sea, who led Israel through the wilderness, who made the sun stand still, I

COMMAND YOU TO LEAVE THIS PLACE. *(Satan begins to back away.)*

**Satan:** All right my friend, but I'll be back. Trust me. I'll be back. *(He exits. Jesus faces the altar and bows his head. He prays silently for a few moments and then leaves the other way.)*

# Drama Five

**Characters:**

    **Jesus of Nazareth:** Young man in late 20s or early 30s. He is dressed in clean blue jeans and a shirt.

    **Satan:** Well dressed, sports coat and tie or three-piece suit, bowler hat or straw hat and walking stick.

    The drama is set in the Garden of Gethsemane. Jesus comes out on stage alone and he talks to the audience as though they are Peter, James and John. This way the congregation will feel a part of what is going on. When Jesus begins to pray, he is joined by Satan, and when Jesus is done praying, he looks up and acknowledges Satan.

**Jesus:** *(He walks out on stage and turns to the audience.)* Peter, James and John, the sorrow in my heart is so great that I can barely stand it. Stay here and watch with me. I will be back in a few moments. *(Jesus proceeds on and kneels at the communion rail. He prays silently for a few moments and then Satan walks on stage and sits down. Then Jesus prays out loud.)* Father, if it is possible, take this cup of suffering from me! Yet not what I want, but what you want. Amen. *(He looks up and sees Satan.)* Working late I see.

**Satan:** Satan's work is never done. I work late all the time. Hey kid, how are you doing?

**Jesus:** Pretty good.

**Satan:** Hey, don't play games with me. We've been through too much together. You can level with me.

**Jesus:** You know when you talk like that it almost sounds like we are on the same side. It kind of sounds like you genuinely care about me. You have a great deal of potential. You probably could have been arch-angel instead of Gabriel and Michael.

**Satan:** Are you kidding, I was the best. Those two couldn't even polish my halo, when I had one. And I do care about you.

**Jesus:** You do, huh?

**Satan:** You bet I do. Look, what are you now, 30 or 31?

**Jesus:** I'm 33 actually.

**Satan:** Wow, has it been that long? I guess what they say is true.

**Jesus:** What's that?

**Satan:** Time flies when you're having fun. It seems like just yesterday that I met you out in the wilderness.

**Jesus:** It was a long time ago.

**Satan:** You have been a worthy opponent. The best I've ever faced.

**Jesus:** You know what is tragic about all of this?

**Satan:** What's that?

**Jesus:** I really like you. You can be a warm, caring person. I's too bad you went bad.

**Satan:** Hey, don't feel sorry for me, kid. I made my bed and now I will lie in it.

**Jesus:** But it is not too late to change.

**Satan:** *(He laughs.)* You've got to be kidding. It's way too late for me, but it's not too late for you.

**Jesus:** What do you mean?

**Satan:** I mean you are only 33 years old. That's too young to die. Think of all the stuff that you have missed out on. Think about all you will be giving up.

**Jesus:** And just what will I be giving up?

**Satan:** The sunrise. No more beautiful part of the day. One moment it's dark and cold, the next moment, the first rays of the new day break through. It's fantastic. No more sunsets. Think about those beautiful colors. The reds, oranges, lavenders. No more walks on a spring day. Never again will you hear the laugh of children, experience the joy of a wedding, or feel the touch of another human being. After tomorrow, all it will be is a cold tomb, darkness, emptiness, death. Death is not good at any age, but especially at such a young age. I don't understand it.

**Jesus:** Don't understand what?

**Satan:** Why God is doing this to you. It's not fair. You're a good man. You never hurt anyone. All you've ever done is help people. Everyone who really knows you, likes you. I don't know if you've got an enemy in the world.

**Jesus:** Tell that to Caiaphas, Herod and Pilate.

**Satan:** But they don't know you. If they knew you, they'd be on your side. It's just a darn shame. You could have been somebody special. You could have made a real name for yourself. Now you will just be another good man who got crushed by the system. I hate to think about it. The price you are going to pay is awfully high. I don't think it's fair, I don't think it's right. I don't think God should place this burden on you.

**Jesus:** But it is a burden that I have taken on myself. No one forced me.

**Satan:** But if God really loved you, he would not make you go through this. He wouldn't demand your death. It's not fair.

**Jesus:** Where is it written that life is fair?

**Satan:** Wait a minute. You know I could help you.

**Jesus:** How?

**Satan:** Look, as I was coming up here I was about 15 minutes ahead of a group that is coming out here to arrest you. I know a back way out of here.

**Jesus:** A back way, huh?

**Satan:** Yes, very few know about it. If we hurry, we can get out of here before that posse arrives. We can beat it up into the hills. They'd never find you. Come on, it's not too late.

**Jesus:** I'd really like to.

**Satan:** Well, what's stopping you? All you have to do is put one foot in front of the other and follow me. We'll be out of here in a flash.

**Jesus:** In a flash, huh?

**Satan:** In a flash. Trust me.

**Jesus:** *(He turns away and walks back to face the audience.)* Peter, James, John! Wake up! How could you fall asleep now? I need you. I need your help. I need your support. I need your prayers. My spirit is willing, but my flesh is weak. Help me, I'm a human being like you. Please help me. Please! *(He walks back and kneels down at the altar or communion rail and prays.)* My Father, if this cup of suffering cannot be taken away unless I drink it, your will be done.

**Satan:** Scared, huh.

**Jesus:** Very.

**Satan:** Look. What good thing can come from suffering? If God really loved you, he wouldn't make you suffer.

**Jesus:** I know that the Father loves me.

**Satan:** Wait a minute. I'm no father. But I know one thing. If I were a father, I would not put any of my children through the kind of hell you're going through.

**Jesus:** You wouldn't, huh?

**Satan:** Come on. It doesn't make any sense. You bring children into the world because you love them. You don't bring children into the world to be cruel to them. This is terribly cruel. I can't believe it. And they call me evil! God is the evil one in all of this. If God is in control, if he is really in control, why is he letting this happen?

**Jesus:** Because of his love.

**Satan:** His love, huh? He's got a funny way of showing love.

**Jesus:** Tell me, what is a good parent like?

**Satan:** Well, let's see. A good parent is one who loves his children. Who provides for his children. Who gives them what they need when they need it. Who will do whatever he can for his kids. A good parent is one who never lets his children suffer. In fact, a good parent would rather die instead of letting anything happen to his children. Let's see. I guess that's about it.

**Jesus:** What about discipline?

**Satan:** I don't believe in it myself. Punishment has always seemed so cruel. So unfair.

**Jesus:** I am not talking about punishment, I'm talking about discipline.

**Satan:** What's the difference?

**Jesus:** To discipline is to lead children in the right way. Sometimes that requires stern measures. To be disciplined is to be obedient. God calls on us to be obedient, to be disciplined.

**Satan:** What does that have to do with your death?

**Jesus:** I will be taking the discipline that all humanity deserves for their disobedience, for their undisciplined natures. I will pay the price. And then everyone will be free from the power of sin and death.

**Satan:** That's too much of a price to pay, even for you.

**Jesus:** When you love someone, really love them, no price is too high.

**Satan:** I admire your nobility, but you can accomplish much more if we get out of here now.

**Jesus:** I am here to accomplish what the Father sent me to do and that's all. No matter what.

**Satan:** Even if it means your own death?

**Jesus:** *(He pauses for a while.)* Yes, even if it means my own death.

**Satan:** Well, you are more foolish than I thought.

**Jesus:** What?

**Satan:** I mean you are a fool. You don't have to do what God wants you to do. Assert yourself. Follow me and I will get you out of this. Just throw in your lot with me and we can beat this. Don't be a fool.

**Jesus:** A fool, huh?

**Satan:** Yes, a fool. Don't throw away everything that I can give you. Just put this cross business out of your head.

**Jesus:** I must do as the Father wants.

**Satan:** Be a fool if you want to. But don't go to the cross. You can't, because it will be the end.

**Jesus:** The end of what?

**Satan:** Ahhh. The end of your life.

**Jesus:** You mean the end of your reign of terror.

**Satan:** I don't know what you are talking about.

**Jesus:** You are good, really good.

**Satan:** What do you mean?

**Jesus:** I mean all of your concern, your care. It was meaningless. You are a fraud. You fed me that line to keep me from the cross so that you wouldn't lose. You don't care about anyone or anything except yourself. I can't believe how good you are. You acted like you really cared.

**Satan:** Hey, you can't blame a guy for trying. Look, you fool, drop it. Give up this noble, but misguided fight and join me. Together we can defeat God. We can take his kingdom by force. Together we can stop him. We can destroy him.

**Jesus:** *(He kneels down and prays.)*

**Satan:** Go ahead and pray if you want to, you fool. You think God is listening to you? You think he cares? God has deserted you. He has abandoned you. He has left you to your own devices. *(He looks around, then back at Jesus.)* Come on, they are almost here. It's not too late. We can still make it. If God really loved you, he wouldn't put you through this. Come on. *(Jesus gets up and goes down and faces the* *congregation while Satan keeps talking.* Where are you going? You're going the wrong way.

**Jesus:** Peter, James, John. Get up. The hour is at hand. Here is my betrayer. *(Jesus then walks off the stage.)*

**Satan:** I don't believe it. He's a fool. What an idiot. I gave him a way out. COME BACK YOU FOOL. I don't know what to do. This has never happened before. Calm down, don't get excited. You are still the best. But what if he continues to resist? I'm lost. Relax, he won't. No one can stand up to you. But he's done so well so far. I mean, it's all over. Take it easy, he's just rattled your confidence a little bit, that's all. Don't let it get to you. But if he succeeds. I mean, no more power, no more leverage, no more control. It's all over, that's all. What will I do? Get a grip on yourself. You still have another shot. You've got the rest of tonight and tomorrow. All night without sleep, all the pain, he'll crack. But it's getting late. I don't have much time left. You always work best under pressure. Get hold of yourself. If you don't, you'll be good to no one. But what if he makes it? What if he can withstand me? Then I'm lost, right? Don't think like that. But what if he does withstand me? Don't worry. If he withstands you, you can still get even. How? By taking *(He looks at the audience.)* as many of them with you as you can. *(He leaves.)*

# Drama Six

**Characters:**

**Jesus of Nazareth:** mid 30s, dressed in blue jeans, but not shabbily dressed. He might wear a black robe to symbolize death.

**Satan:** Neatly dressed. He wears a dark three-piece suit, bowler hat and walking stick.

The drama begins with Jesus standing in front of a large cross. He may rest his arms on the crossbeam or just leave his arms at his sides. Satan is seated in the audience.

**Satan:** *(From the audience.)* If you are the Son of God, save yourself. *(He walks down in front of Jesus, then looks at the audience.)* He saved others, *(To Jesus.)* let him save himself. Why Messiah, all you have to do is come down from there and we will believe in you. *(To the audience.)* Right? Of course I'm right. Painful, huh? It would seem to me that if you were truly God's son, he wouldn't let this happen to you. Are you sure that you got everything straight? Maybe you didn't understand what God was saying to you. That's it. You didn't hear him right. This kind of makes me wonder if you are God's son at all. Doesn't it make you wonder? Hey, what if you are wrong? What if you aren't God's son? What if you are dying for nothing? I don't know, Jesus, I'd want to be pretty sure before I did a thing like this. Are you sure? You better be sure. You know, if you're not sure, just come down from there. Take some time. Think it over. Don't do anything on the spur of the moment.

**Jesus:** Father, forgive them, for they know not what they do.

**Satan:** *(He laughs out loud.)* I don't believe it. I don't believe you. You are so naive, it is unreal. *(He walks right up to Jesus' ear.)* They don't need, they don't want your forgiveness. They don't think they've done anything wrong, so why should they ask for forgiveness. Besides that, how can you forgive them? How can you forgive them for betraying you? Can you really forgive Matthew, James and John? They ran away at Gethsemane. And how can you forgive that blowhard, Peter? "Lord, I'll die with you." How about God? If he doesn't care that you are dying. He doesn't care how you die. If he did, he'd stop this. No, none of them are here. None of them are here because they don't care. The ones you thought were the most faithful, the one you trusted the most, they have left you to die. How can you forgive them? And this crowd. You want to forgive this crowd? Look at Caiaphas over there, he's laughing at you. You want to forgive him? How about

Pilate? He knew all along that you were innocent and he let you die. He sold you out, to save his own political skin. You really want to forgive him? Don't be a fool. You have deluded yourself. People don't care about you. If you only knew. They will use your word to put people, heretics, to death. They will torture people because they don't believe in you. They are going to turn your church into a political football to play their little power games in. They are going to hate anyone who doesn't look at them, and they are going to ignore the poor and the homeless. They will bicker, fight and argue, and ministry will not get done. Is that what you want to die for? Is that the kind of people you want to forgive? I could see you dying if millions would worship you, but you'll be lucky to have a few thousand true believers. Do you think all the people who will attend your church one day are really going to believe in you? If you do, then you are a bigger fool than I thought. *(He pauses for a moment.)* Did you hear that? The thief on this side is making fun of you. Even those who are dying with you think you are a fool. There is no honor among thieves. *(He pauses again.)* Did you hear that? The one on this side wants you to remember him when you come into your kingdom. Oh, that's rich.

**Jesus:** Truly, truly, I say to you, today you will be with me in paradise.

**Satan:** *(He laughs.)* Oh no. Forgiving crooks. What's next? You must be desperate for followers. Look, that crook doesn't really believe in you. He's just covering his bets that's all. There really aren't any atheists in foxholes are there? Listen, this is futile. You, God, you've all lost, so give it up. It's not too late. Come down from there and let's talk things over. This whole ordeal is just too grisly to deal with. I bet it's starting to get more difficult to breathe. Have you ever come close to drowning? Have you ever experienced the feeling of not being able to breathe? It's horrible. And that's what you are going to die from. Your chest muscles will cramp, you won't be able to breathe, and you will suffocate. Or maybe, if you're lucky, you'll have a massive heart attack. You'll begin to feel a tightness in your chest. You'll feel a pain in your jaw and arm, and then it will feel like your chest is exploding. But even worse, what if you are one of the unlucky ones? What if you are one of the ones that stays alive for two or three days? Driven out of your mind with pain. The birds in the air will come and tear off pieces of your flesh. Peck your eyes out. You can avoid all of that, by just coming down from there. Follow me and I will make it easy for you. *(He turns and looks at the audience.)* Oh, this is horrible. Too horrible for me. *(He turns back to Jesus.)* Look, your mother is here. She's come here with John Mark, the beloved disciple. Your poor mother. To have to witness this. I just don't know. Look, if not for your sake, then for hers. Come down from there. Spare her.

**Jesus:** Woman, behold your son. Behold your mother.

**Satan:** It almost brings a tear to my eye. I think it is wonderful that you can think of others ahead of yourself. First the crowd, then the crook and now your mother. You know, she really doesn't care about you. That's right. She thinks you're crazy. And she is right. Oh, you don't believe it? Think back. Let's see, it was just after our little encounter in the wilderness. You had just picked the 12 apostles and you were in your hometown. You were teaching and your mother and your brothers came to get you. You know why they came? Because they thought you were crazy. They thought you needed to be put away. Thought you needed to be chained up, like an animal. They were against all this from the very beginning. They thought you were crazy. And I can see why. Some people think they are Alexander the Great or Napoleon, or Teddy Roosevelt, but you, you think you are the Son of God, the Messiah. You're crazy. Come down from there and we'll get you some help. That's why your mother is here. She knows you need help. Come on. There is no shame in recognizing your problems. Just face them and a few months of care and home cooking and you'll be a new man. Do you know what she is going through? Why make her suffer? There is nothing harder than burying one of your own children. And that's what you are going to make that poor woman do. Bury her firstborn son. Think of her. Think of what this will do to her. If you really loved her, if you really were a good son, you'd come down from there and take her home. The pain is starting to get to you, isn't it?

**Jesus:** My God, my God, why have you forsaken me?

**Satan:** You're right, he has forsaken you. The one who you said loved everyone, has left you here all alone to die. What kind of God is that? I thought God was love. I thought God was care. I thought God was compassionate. God is barbaric, hypocritical, a phony. He doesn't love you. He doesn't love anyone but himself. So forget it. Death is the one thing you have to do alone. No one can do it for you. Yesterday you talked so big about the love of God. How God could see you through anything and everything. Well, where is God now? He has left you to die in this hell all alone. Look, let me help you. Just come down from there and I'll take care of you. You can trust me. I won't let you down like God has done. Look, if you come down from there now, you'll never have to be alone again. Just think about the mistake you are making. Look, go home to Nazareth. Go back to work in the carpenter shop. Build some tables, chairs and chests. Get married, raise a family. A wife and kids would be a great comfort to you in your old age. This is folly. You're being ridiculous.

**Jesus:** I thirst.

**Satan:** I bet you do. Haven't had a thing to drink since last night. Your mouth must feel like a piece of sandpaper. Your tongue is swollen and it sticks to the roof of your mouth. Yes, some water would taste good, wouldn't it? Cool, fresh, clear, thirst quenching water. It's all yours. All you have to do is come down from there. I know you can't go on too much longer like this. You don't want to die, at least not like this. How about some wine? I've got a couple of bottles we can share. I've got a Bordeaux bottled in '23. And a white Zinfandel bottled in '18. Smooth as cream. Just the tonic you need. Now come on. Let's get out of here. This whole business is doing no one any good. Just forget it all. Look, I'm trying to help you. I'm trying to show you the best way. And your death is not the best way. Look, eventually they are going to take you down from here and throw you in a cold, empty tomb. Is that how you want to end up? Thrown out like yesterday's garbage? Come on, you are smarter than that. You've got more brains than that. Use them.

**Jesus:** It is finished.

**Satan:** Nooooooo! Nothing is finished. You're not done with me, friend. It's not finished by a long shot. The worst is still to come. In a little while they are going to come and break your legs. They're going to take that big sledge down there and smash your legs. That will cause you to sag down and make your breathing even more difficult. You don't know what pain and terror are like until you can't get your breath. You want to scream but there is no air to let out. You want to curse the pain, but you can't. No, it's not finished. You're not finished. I won't let you be finished. You think I gave up everything, you think I gave up being a part of the kingdom to end up like this? Broken on some stupid tree? No, not me. I hate you. I hate you for not being selfish, for not being greedy, for not being lazy, for not being disobedient. I hate you. But it is not finished. You come down from there. You come down here and fight like a man. You don't want to be up there, you phony Messiah. No one can love God that much. No one can love people that much. Why are you so different than anyone else? What keeps you up there? I have tempted you with my best stuff. Others have given in to me, why not you? What keeps you up there? Nothing I have tried has worked. I can't understand it. But it isn't finished. Not yet. No way.

**Jesus:** Father, into your hands I commend my spirit.

**Satan:** What? What did you say? *(He lifts Jesus' head. He feels for a pulse.)* He's gone. He's dead. I don't believe it. I've lost. I, I, I just don't know what to do. It's starting to get dark. Looks like a real bad storm brewing. I never dreamed he would make it. I don't know what made him stay up there. They were just ordinary spikes. He could have removed them. All he had to do was assert his power. There must have been something else holding him up there. I know it was his love. His love for you. I never realized how powerful a force love ocan be. What? *(He turns toward the cross and back to the crowd.)* Did you hear that soldier? "Truly, this man was the Son of God." He was the Son of God. Do you know that? Do you believe that? I don't think you do. I think you doubt him and everything that's ever been said about him. And you know that. That's when I can work the best, when you doubt. I may have lost him, but I'll be back to get you. *(He exits.)*